Christmas

Tim Wood

Photographs by Maggie Murray
Illustrations by Sheila Jackson

Christmas at Rosebury

A & C Black · London

Acknowledgements

The author and publisher would like to thank Gill Tanner for
loaning items from her collections for photography. They
would also like to thank Doris Cooksley; Violet Jones; Suella
Postles, Curator Brewhouse Yard Museum, Nottingham;
Nottingham Museum Staff; Margaret Evans, Sarah Edwards
and Richard Davis at Aberystwyth Yesterday; and especially
Jane and Kate Hartoch.

Photographs by Maggie Murray except for: p12 (left), 26
(right), 27 (top), 28, Beamish Open Air Museum; p22 (top),
British Library; p11 (bottom), 14 (bottom), 15 (top and bottom),
18 (bottom), 19 (bottom), 23 (top), 25, Christmas Archives; p5
(top), 10 (top), 11 (top), 13 (top), 21 (top and bottom), 23
(bottom), 29 (top), Mary Evans Picture Library; p4 Sally and
Richard Greenhill; p5 (bottom) Salvation Army; Cover (inset)
Illustrated London News

Published by A & C Black (Publishers) Limited
35 Bedford Row
London WC1R 4JH
© 1991 A & C Black (Publishers) Limited

ISBN 0 7136 3350 6

A CIP catalogue record for this book is available
from the British Library.

Filmset by August Filmsetting, Haydock, St Helens
Printed in Italy by Amadeus

Contents

What does Christmas mean to you?

Do you celebrate Christmas? It's one of the most important Christian festivals of the year, and to many people it's a very special time. Even if you don't celebrate, you probably have a holiday, see the Christmas trees and decorations in the shops, and watch Christmas programmes on television.

Have you ever thought where all our Christmas traditions come from? One hundred and fifty years ago, British children did not hang up their stockings on Christmas Eve. Hardly anyone ate turkey for Christmas dinner or had a Christmas tree in their house. There were no crackers and no one had heard of Santa Claus.

Even when your great grandparents were young, at the turn of the century, Christmas was very different from the way it is today. Many people did not celebrate it at all. Some people didn't even have a holiday – for them, Christmas was exactly like any other day of the year.

◀ This illustration drawn at the turn of the century shows the Christmas meal being eaten in a very rich home. Notice that although there are many dishes on the table there is no turkey. There are also no crackers.

▲ A Christmas party for poor children, given by the Salvation Army. At the turn of the century many people had no money to spend at Christmas and received no help from the state.

◀ A modern family enjoying their Christmas dinner.

The origins of Christmas

The Christmas festival celebrates the birth of Jesus. But many of our Christmas customs began long before Jesus was born. They came from earlier festivals which had nothing to do with the Christian Church.

In ancient times, when people did not understand what caused the seasons, many had mid-winter festivals when the days were shortest and the sunlight weakest.

People believed that their ceremonies would give the sun back its power. The Romans, for example, held the festival of Saturnalia round about 25 December. They decorated their homes with evergreens to remind Saturn, their harvest god, to return the following spring. They also gave each other small presents. Many mid-winter festivals included a feast.

bay

yew

▲ Evergreens were used as decorations in ancient times. They were thought to have magical powers because they stayed green throughout the winter.

► Mistletoe was used by the ancient Celts to make charms.

mistletoe

ivy

▲ The Christmas wreath probably came from the victory wreath which was given to successful generals in Roman times.

3 kings

◀ A kissing bush was made at Christmas from a bunch of evergreens with a sprig of mistletoe in the middle. Any girl kissed under the bush was sure of good luck and a happy marriage.

holly

▲ Holly was used by early Christians as a symbol of the crucifixion of Christ. The pointed tips of the leaves represented Christ's crown of thorns; the berries drops of His blood.

▶ Candles were often used in the past to light the winter darkness. Christians used them on advent wreaths which they made to celebrate the coming of Christ. One candle was lit on each of the four Sundays before Christmas. A fifth candle, which was usually red, was lit on Christmas Day to symbolise Jesus. Some people still make these advent wreaths.

presents

◀ The old tradition of giving mid-winter presents was adopted by the early Christians. It fitted the pattern started by the three Wise Men who gave gifts to the baby Jesus.

Some of these old customs and traditions were adopted by early Christians as part of their celebrations of Jesus' birthday. The word Christmas actually comes from 'Christ's Mass', the church service which was held to celebrate the birth of Christ. We are not sure when it all began, but we do know that by about 1100 Christmas had become one of the most important religious festivals in the Christian year.

Many of the old mid-winter customs and traditions gradually became part of the Christmas celebrations. In Victorian times some new ideas, such as Santa Claus, Christmas cards and crackers, were added to make the Christmas we know today.

Time-line

	pre-1880s	1880s	1890s	1900s	1910s	1920
		Great great grandparents were born		**Great grandparents were born**		
Important events	**1870** Alexander Graham Bell invents telephone	**1888** Dunlop invents pneumatic tyre	**1890** Moving pictures start **1896** First modern Olympic Games	**1901** Queen Victoria dies. Edward VII becomes King **1903** Wright brothers fly first plane	**1910** George V becomes King **1914–18** World War I	**1926** Gene Strike in Britain
Christmas dates	**1840** Prince Albert puts up the first Christmas tree in Britain at Windsor Castle **1841** *Punch* magazine recommends people to give generously at Christmas **1843** *A Christmas Carol* written by Charles Dickens ● The first Christmas card produced for Sir Henry Cole **1846** The first Christmas cracker	**1880** Service of Nine Lessons and Carols introduced by Bishop Benson at Truro, Cornwall	Winter sports become fashionable **1891** Publication in England of 'The Night Before Christmas' by Clement Clarke Moore **1894** 'Santa Claus Distribution Fund' founded in London to give presents and clothing to poor children **1898** First advertisements for Christmas presents appear in *The Times* ● Turkeys become popular for Christmas dinner	By 1900 Boxing Day is a holiday throughout England and Wales **1901** Meccano invented	**1911** 1,400,000 people are employed in domestic service and so are unable to go home for Christmas **1914** Christmas presents of tobacco and chocolate given to the troops in the trenches ● Troops from both sides celebrate Christmas together	'Hornby' tr sets first produced ● Mass production toys

8

This time-line shows some of the important events since your great grandparents were children, and some of the events and inventions which have changed Christmas and how we celebrate it.

...ndparents ...ere born	Parents were born				You were born	
...30s	1940s	1950s	1960s	1970s	1980s	1990s
...dward ...dicates. ...e VI ...es King. ...t ...ion ...asts ...orld ...starts	1941 Penicillin successfully tested 1945 World War II ends 1947 First supersonic plane	1952 Elizabeth II becomes Queen 1959 Yuri Gagarin first man in space	1969 Neil Armstrong first man on the moon 	1973 Britain enters the Common Market	1981 First successful space shuttle flight	1990s
...Toys' ...oduced ...rst royal ...mas ...ge is ...cast on ...dio by ...eorge V 	During World War II toys are scarce. Many people make their own or buy second-hand toys 1942 'White Christmas' is sung by Bing Crosby. It becomes the largest selling record of all time with over 30,000,000 copies sold, plus 100,000,000 cover versions made by other artists 1946 First Christmas tree is put up in Trafalgar Square, London	Public services, such as the railways, begin to close for Christmas ● Christmas decorations and cards become big business. Television advertising begins. Christmas becomes 'commercial' 1956 First royal Christmas message is broadcast on television by Queen Elizabeth II 1956 Clean Air Act leads to the gradual disappearance of open fires and chimneys	Post Office (then the GPO) stops deliveries over the Christmas Holiday (from noon on Christmas Eve) ● Most industries allow a week's holiday for their workers at Christmas	Christmas decorations become a multi-million pound industry. 'Craze' toys made by American companies such as Fisher-Price, Mattel and Hasbro begin to dominate the toy market. Many are featured in television programmes and widely advertised	1984 'Do They Know It's Christmas?' by Band Aid becomes the Christmas hit record. The money raised goes to the Ethiopian Relief Fund	

9

Christmas customs

Many of the Christmas customs which were traditional in great grandma's time have now died out.

Different regions had their own special Christmas ceremonies. In the West Country, people drank a toast to the cider apple trees with hot cider punch. This ceremony of 'wassailing' was supposed to encourage the trees to produce lots of apples in the following year.

In Hertfordshire, widows went 'A-Thomasing' round the houses on St Thomas' Day (21 December), asking for gifts. In certain parts of Scotland, pupils locked their teacher out of the classroom and then bargained with him or her to give them a Christmas holiday.

▲ Poorer people often went carol singing to get money for themselves. Rival bands sometimes fought each other. Hundreds of years ago, carols were performed at other important religious festivals, such as Easter.

A new tradition which grew up at the end of the Victorian period was that of going home for the Christmas holiday. The railways provided cheap, speedy travel for people who worked away from home and for young middle-class boys who had been away at boarding schools. Many poorer people moved into large towns for Christmas, hoping to find casual work or to get hand-outs from charities.

◀ These children looked at a case of old family photographs and documents in their local library. They found Christmas cards from the turn of the century, and a diary of the Christmas holidays in 1914 written as a homework exercise in a schoolbook.

Those who were very poor could not afford to travel. Others, such as domestic servants, were not allowed to go home. Many people in public service, such as railway workers, did not get a holiday.

▲ A picture from a children's book showing the traditional ceremony of dragging in the Yule log. Many people burned one large log through the Christmas period. Some people now eat a chocolate 'Yule log' cake at Christmas.

◄ Very poor people collecting free coal from a parish officer to help them through the cold Christmas period. Giving charity at Christmas was one custom which became more popular in Victorian times.

Christmas shopping

We are used to buying food and presents for Christmas in large supermarkets or in chain stores. In great grandma's day there were few department stores, and those were mainly in the large cities. Great grandma probably did her shopping in lots of small stores.

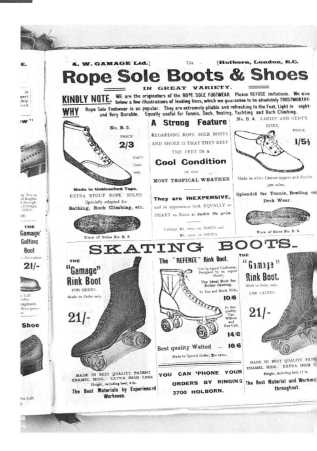

▲ Gamages store in London had one of the largest mail order catalogues.

▲ By the turn of the century many shops put up special Christmas displays. This display has been reconstructed in a museum, using some original Victorian decorations.

In a rich household some of the heavy or boring shopping was done by servants. Rich people could avoid the crowded trams and horse-drawn omnibuses by having their goods brought from the shops by delivery boys riding bicycles or driving carts. Many middle-class people found it more convenient to buy some of their presents through the mail order catalogues which were just becoming popular.

THE COMPLIMENTS OF THE SEASON

LIKE THE CUCKOO WITH BUT ONE SONG.

▲ This early Christmas card shows a street trader selling toys.
People who were too poor to buy even these cheap toys might make their own.

▼ Rag and bottle shops bought second-hand goods and reusable rubbish. The poster encouraged people to earn a few extra pennies for Christmas.

CHRISTMAS MERRY-MAKING
AND
How to Enjoy it !

Games are really enjoyed when the necessaries, Puddings, Beef, &c., are paid for by saving up all your Rags, Bones and Lumber, and bringing them to This Shop.

Poorer people could not afford to shop in large stores. They bought their food in markets or from street traders, and their presents from penny bazaars or pedlars.

The unemployed, old or very poor could not afford to shop at all. They may have spent Christmas in a workhouse. These could be grim places but, thanks to money collected by various charities, the inmates usually received a special Christmas meal, a card, and perhaps even a small present. These gifts were often accompanied by sermons and lectures about the dangers of drink and the virtue of hard work.

13

At the turn of the century, people who were very rich might have owned several huge houses and kept a small army of servants to look after them. People who were poor might have lived in one room, had no inside toilet and shared a cold water tap with several other families. What people ate for Christmas depended on how well-off they were. A rich household would consume huge quantities of food. A poor family might not eat anything special at all.

In a richer household the cook planned and presented her menus long before Christmas Day. Puddings, cakes and mincemeat were prepared several weeks ahead. Turkey, which was fashionable but not yet considered the traditional food by most people, might have been the main course.

▲ Sugar mice were often hung from the Christmas tree as edible decorations or put into children's stockings. These children learned how to make them from icing sugar mixed with egg white and a few drops of cochineal for colouring.

▼ Great grandma probably made her pudding on 'Stir-up Sunday' at the start of Advent. The pudding was stirred from east to west in honour of the three Wise Men. Every member of the family stirred the pudding and made a wish.

14

Poorer people ate goose or chicken. Very poor people ate rabbit or pig's head. Many poorer people joined goose clubs to save a little money each week. At Christmas the money was used to buy geese for all the club members. The geese were different sizes so, to make sure everyone was treated fairly, tickets for the birds were drawn out of a hat.

Doris Cooksley, who was born in 1900, remembers:

'We usually had a chicken for our Christmas dinner. Ma made a Christmas pudding for each of us. There were nine of us children so she cooked eleven puddings in the copper. Dad stayed up all night stoking the fire.'

▲ The goose market. Poorer people could always wait until the last minute to find a bargain from a stall-holder desperate to sell all his birds before Christmas.

◄ Christmas puddings were sometimes cooked in the copper which was usually used for washing clothes. Plum pudding and mince pies have been popular since the Middle Ages. Mince pies, sometimes called wayfarers' pies, were given to Christmas visitors.

Christmas cards

The first Christmas card was produced in 1843 for Sir Henry Cole who had 1000 of them printed to sell in his London art shop. Most people sent letters or made their own cards. It was not until after World War I that cards were mass-produced and became cheap enough for almost everyone to send.

Many early Christmas cards showed pictures of nymphs and fairies, or summer scenes. Very few had the pictures of snow, Santa Claus, robins and stagecoaches which are usually on cards today.

Richer people could buy expensive cards which were almost works of art, costing over five pounds, a large sum of money in those days. Many children made their own.

▼ Doris Cooksley told the children 'We made all our Christmas cards. Ma made each of us send one card to the same cousin each year'. The children tried making their own Victorian-style Christmas cards.

▼ They found that they could make beautiful cards which looked quite complicated from a few simple materials.

▲ Christmas cards at the turn of the century came in all shapes and sizes. Some were very elaborate and opened like concertinas. The one in the centre of the bottom row is the oldest. It was printed on fine leather. The postcard was written over 20 years later.

◄ After Christmas many people stuck their cards into albums. The children were surprised at how few of the cards in this album showed Christmas scenes.

The introduction of the 'Penny Post' in 1840 and the invention of the railway meant that people could send their letters and cards anywhere in the country for just one penny. At the turn of the century the postman even delivered cards on Christmas Day.

Some charities quickly realised how a Christmas message could cheer people in trouble. In 1881 the Christmas Letter Mission sent 300,000 Christmas cards to people in workhouses, prisons and hospitals. Each envelope was marked 'A Christmas Letter for You' and was put on the pillow by one of the staff after dark on Christmas Eve.

Decorations

Although it was possible to buy certain types of Christmas decoration at the turn of the century, most people made their own. The Victorians adopted the old Twelfth Night tradition of decorating their houses and churches with evergreens. In the north of England, barrel hoops decorated with evergreens were hung on the walls. Mottoes made from everlasting flowers and mosses giving Christmas messages such as 'Pray As You Walk In' or 'A Thousand Welcomes', were hung up. Some of the decorations took weeks to make.

Even poor people could gather evergreens from the countryside. Beds were decorated with holly to keep away evil spirits. People wrote their mottoes in chalk around the fireplace and made paper chains from coloured paper and flour paste glue. They put candles in glass jars to light the way to the outside toilet. Doris told the children who interviewed her:

'We made all our own decorations, such as paper chains. We started in November and kept them in a cupboard till Christmas Eve'.

◄ A modern Christmas tree with decorations from 1900. At the turn of the century trees were often decorated on Christmas Eve.

The most important decoration was the Christmas tree made popular by Prince Albert, husband of Queen Victoria. In Germany, where he was born, Christmas trees had been used for a long time. The trees were lit with small candles fixed into metal candle holders. These could be quite dangerous and, in some rich houses a servant was always ready to put out the flames if the tree caught fire.

▲ Victorian candle holders and cake decorations.

▲ Collecting evergreens was fun for the better-off, but for the poor or unemployed it was a useful source of extra income at Christmas time. This trade was called 'Christmasing'.

◄ This photograph was taken in 1910.

19

The children tried carol singing, accompanie by a type of organ called a harmonium.

Christmas Eve at the turn of the century was a very busy day indeed. There was plenty of work to prepare for the following day.

Like many other children, Doris went carol singing with her sisters on Christmas Eve. The money they collected was used to buy useful things in the New Year.

Later in the evening some families went to a midnight service at their local church. Doris and her family stayed in. She told the children:

'We put up all our decorations and dressed the tree on Christmas Eve. All of us helped. Then before we went to bed Ma read us a story and we sang some carols while she played the piano.'

▲ The back cover of a carol book. Can you spot the Christmas robin in the picture?

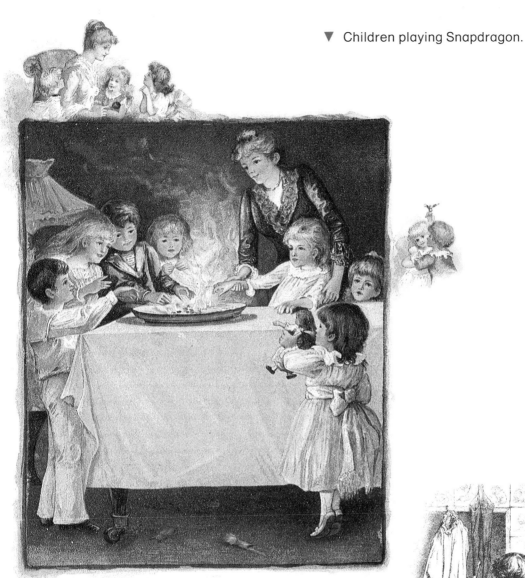

Some children still played the traditional game of Snapdragon. Raisins were put in a bowl and soaked in brandy. Then an adult set light to them. The lights were turned out and everyone took turns to snatch raisins from the flames. The class decided that this sounded rather dangerous!

Once the games were over, the children went upstairs and hung up their stockings. Doris remembers:

'We six girls slept in the same room, three in each bed. We hung our stockings on the mantlepiece, or tied them to the bedpost.'

▲ On Christmas Eve, great grandma hung up her best black stockings or a nightdress.

21

Father Christmas

The children were surprised to discover that Santa Claus is quite a newcomer to Christmas. He is a mixture of two legendary people. One was Father Christmas, a character in traditional mummers' plays. Father Christmas had no sleigh, no reindeer and no presents for children. He just represented a spirit of celebration and joy.

European legends tell of St Nicholas who was a real-life bishop in Turkey and became the patron saint of children. He was said to visit European children on the eve of his saint's day (5 December). In Dutch legends he was called Sinter Klaas. He rode a white horse and came down chimneys to put presents into the shoes of those children who had been good. He left a birch rod for those who had been bad.

▲ Santa Claus was quickly adopted by several Victorian charities. He even had his own paper, the 'Santa Claus Gazette'. In 1910, the 'Santa Claus Workers' League' distributed 10,000 presents to poor people.

▼ The class learned about the origin of Santa Claus from a real expert. They discovered that the custom of leaving a mince pie for Santa and sprouts for his reindeer began in Victorian times.

◀ Earlier pictures showed Santa in many different ways. People had not decided exactly what he looked like.

▼ By 1920 Santa Claus was painted as he appears today. He soon became a useful advertising symbol.

CHATTERBOX

The Santa Claus we now know seems to have been born in America. The Sinter Klaas legend was taken to the USA by European immigrants. The Americans adopted him and, over the years, some of his habits changed – his visits, for instance, moved from 5 December to Christmas Eve.

In his popular poem, 'The Night Before Christmas', the American poet Clement Clarke Moore gave Santa a home near the North Pole and a sleigh drawn by reindeer. This created the character we know today. By 1870 this new Santa Claus had reached Britain and merged with our own Father Christmas.

Christmas Day

On Christmas morning, children woke early and opened their stockings in a state of great excitement. They had far fewer presents than you have, but they expected less. Many children thought themselves lucky to have one toy or game, or some hand-me-down clothes. Doris remembered:

'One year we got some wooden building bricks. It was only years later that I realised they were our old bricks which Dad had repainted to make them look new! It didn't matter – we still loved them.'

▼ Books were given as 'improving presents' for children. Many popular children's books told little stories with a moral.

▲ The children were astonished at how few presents were in great grandma's stocking. Doris's stocking always contained a halfpenny, an apple or an orange, a bag of sweets and a small present such as a rag doll, a book or a game.

After stockings had been opened, many people went to a church service. Then it was time for Christmas dinner. In a rich household this was a magnificent feast served by the butler and maids. In ordinary houses it was a large meal eaten round the big kitchen table. Poor people, who had no oven, took their food to the baker's shop to have it cooked in the oven there. Then they carried their hot meal home or ate it in the street.

After dinner, rich children might have more presents to open. In some households, extra presents were kept for Boxing Day. There was no television in those days. On Christmas afternoon and evening, people had to make their own entertainment. Children played with their toys or played family games such as 'Flip the Kipper' or 'Hunt the Slipper', or board games such as Ludo.

TOM SMITH'S · ARTISTIC · CRACKERS
❋ FOR ❋
TABLE DECORATION.

4313
80/- per doz. boxes, 6 in a box

4692
53/- per doz. boxes
12 in a box

4318. 92/6 per doz. boxes, 6 in a box

4690
46/- per doz. boxes
12 in a box

4306
70/- per doz. boxes
6 in a box

4688
40/- per doz. boxes, 12 in a box
Assorted colours

4315
81/6 per doz. boxes, 6 in a box

4316. 84/- per doz. boxes, 6 in a box

4304
66/- per doz. boxes
6 in a box

4687
31/- per doz. boxes
12 in a box.

4696

4301

▲ Crackers were invented in 1846 by Tom Smith, a sweet-maker.
He decided he could sell more sweets if he wrapped them in
a package which went bang when pulled. The crackers were
even more successful when he added paper hats and trinkets.

25

Toys

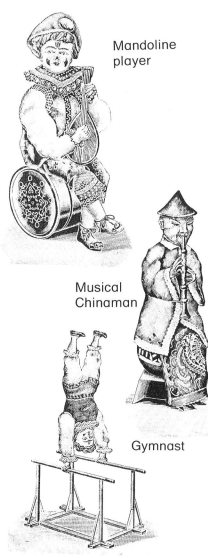

◀ The children tried out some Victorian toys. This picture shows a wooden roundabout, and a kaleidoscope, a toy which has been popular since its invention in 1817.

Mandoline player

Musical Chinaman

Gymnast

Do you have lots of toys you never play with? Do you see advertisements on television which make you want to have the toys they show? At the turn of the century most children had very few toys, and many had no toys at all.

About 150 years ago the toy makers in the United Kingdom made all their toys by hand. Toy making was a very small industry, so there were not many toys to buy. Also there was less advertising encouraging children to want toys. For most people, toys were an expensive luxury. The average child spent about 1p on toys per year, though for this sum he or she could buy a money box, a skipping rope, a box of marbles, a doll or a mousetrap. These were all popular toys at the time. If poor children had any toys, they were home-made.

▲ Mechanical toys, mostly made in Germany, were highly prized. They were driven by clockwork or counterweights. The figures walked or performed tricks. They were very expensive so would only be given to children from rich families.

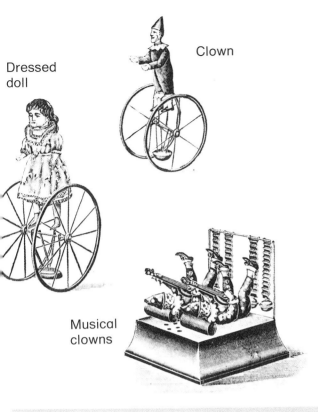

Dressed doll

Clown

Musical clowns

During the last part of Queen Victoria's reign the toy industry began to grow. But it was not until about 1920 that toys, such as Meccano construction kits and Hornby clockwork trains, were mass produced in factories. Hamley's toy shop in London began to have special Christmas displays, and more advertisements for toys began to appear. Board games, and books such as *Little Lord Fauntleroy* and *Black Beauty*, became popular among the rich. Cheaper toys could be bought at Woolworths, or in penny bazaars where everything cost either a halfpenny or a penny.

▼ Boxed games were popular at the turn of the century.

Boxing Day

Boxing Day got its name because this was the day when, by tradition, tradespeople came to collect their Christmas boxes. This tradition began in the Middle Ages when people put money for the poor into alms boxes. The boxes were opened on the day after Christmas.

Over the centuries the custom became an excuse for anyone to collect money from others. Rich people could expect a stream of people, such as servants, traders and shopkeepers, all asking for their Christmas 'box'. They paid them to make sure they would be given good service in the year to come. By the turn of the century Christmas boxes became increasingly unpopular. Many people preferred to give to charities, knowing their money would be spent on people in need.

In many parts of the country traditional mummers' plays, such as the story of St George and the Dragon, were performed on Boxing Day. Pantomimes were very popular treats for children from better-off homes.

Another Boxing Day tradition was for people to take part in, or watch, sports. Boxing Day is the feast of St Stephen, the patron saint of horses. As a result, Boxing Day became associated with horse-racing and hunting. Other sports, such as soccer and rugby, were popular as well.

▲ Boxing Day was also a time when richer people gave charity to people in need. Blankets, clothes and hampers of food were the usual gifts. This magazine picture gives a rather idealised view of charity.

▲ Children tobogganing on Boxing Day.

▼ The children watched a traditional mummers' play. They thought it was very funny.

How to find out more

Start here	To find out about . . .	Who will have . . .
Old people	Christmas at the turn of the century	Old photos, scrap books, old toys
Junk shops	What people bought	Old catalogues, old magazines, old cards
Museums	Old things to look at and possibly to handle	Reconstructed shops, displays
Libraries	● Loan collections ● Reference collections ● Information to help your research ● Local history section	● Books to borrow ● Books, magazines, newspapers ● Useful addresses, guide books, additional reference material ● Newspapers and guides to look at ● Photographs of local people and Christmas events
Local records office	Your area in the past	Local documents, and tapes of local people talking

Who can tell you more?

They can. Use a tape recorder for recording their memories. Handle anything they show you with great care and if they lend you something, label it with their name and keep it somewhere safe

The owner. Specialist shopkeepers are usually very enthusiastic and knowledgeable about their stock. They may know of local people with Christmas collections or be able to give you further contacts and addresses

The curator or the museum's education officer. Many museums have bookshops and a notice board where it would be worth looking for further information. Most museums will have a kit of books which they lend to schools at Christmas. This will be booked well in advance in the winter but will probably be easy to use in the summer

The librarian. The reference librarian. Ask the archivist for the name and address of the local history society

The archivist. These offices are often quite small and very busy. Arrive early or make an appointment.

Places to visit

The following places have displays, reconstructions or exhibitions connected with Christmas. Complete Christmas displays are sometimes put on in the winter at local museums. Ring for details.

Cusworth Hall, Cusworth Land, Doncaster, Humberside. Tel: 0302–782342.
Museum of Childhood, High Street, Edinburgh, Lothian. Tel: 031–225–1131.
Museum of Childhood, Water Street, Menai Bridge, Anglesey, Gwynedd. Tel: 0248–712498.
Museum of Childhood, Cambridge Heath Road, London. Tel: 081–980–2415.
North of England Open Air Museum, Beamish Hall, Beamish, Stanley, Durham. Tel: 0207–31811.
Sudbury Hall, Sudbury, Derbyshire. Tel: 028–378–305.

The following places have displays, reconstructions or exhibitions connected with toys:
Blaise Castle House, Henbury, Bristol. Tel: 0272–506789.
Burrows Toy Museum, York Street, Bath. Tel: 0225–61819.
Dolls and Miniatures, 54 Southside Street, The Barbican, Plymouth. Tel: 0752–663676.
Hamilton House Toy Museum, Church Street, Ashbourne, South Derbyshire. Tel: 0335–44343.
Pollocks Toy Museum, 1 Scala Street, London W1P 1LT. Tel: 071–636–3452.
Toy Museum, 42 Bridge Street Row, Chester, Merseyside. Tel: 0244–316351.
Vintage Toy and Train Museum, Sidmouth, Devon.

Useful addresses

The Christmas Archives. Tel: 0222–341120 The only private collection in the country dedicated entirely to Christmas. They do not expect visitors, but may be a useful source of information. They have a photo library, gigantic Christmas card collection and publish the *Journal of the Society of Nativitists*. Research allowed at educational rates. They supply Christmas materials for films, television and exhibitions. Phone for details of Christmas exhibitions they will be putting on around the country.
Cusworth Hall, Doncaster. Tel:0302–782342. Victorian Christmas family evenings. Morris dancing, carol singing, parlour games, mince pies and punch. Book early.
Haggs Castle, 100 St Andrews Drive, Glasgow. Tel: 041–427–2725. Lots of Victorian and Christmas activities including making cards, presents and food. Booking is essential.

You may also find the *Guardian* newspaper useful. Look for 'What's on for Children' in the Education Section.

Index